The Glue

In Me

POEMS INSPIRED BY GOD
FOR HIS ROYAL FAMILY

DR CONNIE HEMINGWAY

THE GOD IN ME
POEMS INSPIRED BY GOD FOR HIS ROYAL FAMILY

Copyright © 2021 Connie Hemingway
Cover Design Roy Etienne Smith

Dekan Press
an imprint of
MIGMIR Company USA, LLC

www.migmir.us

For Worldwide Distribution
Printed in the U.S.A.

ISBN: 9781952253157
Library of Congress Control Number: 2021909862

TABLE OF CONTENTS

TABLE OF CONTENTS CONT.

DEDICATION

This book is dedicated to my daughter Nyticka and granddaughter, Chloe. I love you both so very much!

To my niece, Rebekah: Thank you for your help and inspiring support through the years.

To Rev. Dr. DeForest Soaries Jr. and First Baptist Church of Lincoln Gardens, I love and appreciate you.

To all of God's royal children: I pray God continues to bless you mightily!

Happy 102nd Birthday in Heaven Momma, I loved you in life and even more in your passing. You are gone but never will you be forgotten. You were all I could have ever asked for in a grandmother, a friend, a confidant, a muse, a teacher and all that I needed for any situation in my life. You were God's angel that he sent to me then and now. I can still sense your moving around and guiding me. I hear that still small voice saying" now! What would God do Connie?"

I sense and feel your presence all the time and the funny little things you used to say, still always come to mind. Ma you would be 102 years old today when you took your last strut across the stage of existence. as we know it down here it was extremely difficult for me and I sure do miss you Girly. My grandmother was born into a horse and buggy world. The year she passed away Barak Obama became

President. She would have never believed it. That fact would have made her so proud.

The very first thing she would have said was now "Connie you sure that boy is colored?" It has for years always amazed me. How speedy the pace of change is? Yesterday's wonder is today's "ho-hum." Her life spanned two wars, the 1918 influenza epidemic, a great depression, the advent of the automobile, the airplane, radio, TV, and space exploration. She remembered when there was no penicillin and when (there was) not, everybody had indoor plumbing. She knew how to pluck a chicken. I saw her do it and she showed me how once.

I was very little and I was amazed. I thought chickens came in saran wrapped packages from the supermarket and not from our own back yard. But, to all of us she made a difference and the difference she made to me, anyway, was staggering. She was my role model for what a woman should and could be. When she died in 2008 January 18, in Princeton New Jersey, many people attended her funeral. Her passing was marked with amazing pomp and circumstance dozens of letters and phone calls attested to the difference she had made in many lives other than mine.

Now, as I approach the time of life she was in during my childhood, I think of her more often. The world which formed my generation is as long gone as her childhood memories. My Gen-X children who are now approaching middle age and their Gen Y offspring can't imagine a world without computers, cell phones, and Instant Messenger, let alone birth control pills, AIDS, and TV ads for Viagra.

The toys I played with as a child are being sold at the flea market as collector's items. The furniture that I grew up with is prized by the young and hip as retro '50's modern. I am walking in the shoes of my grandmother and I only hope I can negotiate the journey half as gracefully and effectively as she did.

To God be all the Glory rest in peace and once again Happy Birthday in Heaven Momma.

Time

There is a rumbling in my belly and a
sound in my inner ear.
Hold it wait a minute God is speaking and
His words are very clear.

"See My daughter I have work for you to
do, there is no time to turn back now.
There are diverse things going on in the
earth, just say hallelujah anyhow.

I did not bring you this far to leave you, or
discourage you in any way.
The ways of a man are not my ways, be
obedient and listen to all I have to say.

The time has come for my Living Water
to be poured out in constant streams.
Your children will prophesy, young
men will see visions old men will dream
dreams.

I have shared with you so many things.
I would not have told you if it were so.
You must reach and teach, tell them of My
goodness, and the wiles of their foe.

Times have never been so crucial, My
people they must be on point and prepared.
When diverse things come to plague
their lives, they must not be left out or
despaired.

I have given you a Word to release to all
that will listen and heed your cry.
I want what is best for all My children and I
am not a man that would lie.

There is coming a time and very soon life
as you once knew it will never be the same.
The things that folks are doing have no
longevity, unless they are doing it in
My name."

Single ladies

Put your hands up in prayer

*L*adies *if you are single there is a reason for* that.

You just have not yet found or met the right cat.

Allow God to be your man.
He is the One with a purpose and a plan.

He will teach you and cuddle you and always be Your friend.
He listens, protects, goes with you, meets you When you get there till the end.

There is no need to suffer from low self-esteem.
You are a daughter of Zion and a beautiful Queen.

Don't allow time to be your enemy
and tell you that you're old.

Have faith in God. He will polish you and keep you like precious gold.

You are better than best and you reign in heavenly places.
This old world will soon be nothing but ashes and devastating traces.

Take your time anything worth having is worth waiting for.
Father God has someone special for you, that will know the score.

You don't have to wonder or wait. Stay on the Lord's side.
He told us in His Word that if we abide in Him, in us He will also abide.

Trust me young ladies taste the Lord for He is Good.
You don't need no brother for the sake of having one. Straight out the hood.
Amen!

Being here

Being here if I had my druthers, I would
leave this old earth and go on to
Heaven today.
But since God sees fit to keep me here, in
and through Him I'll go on my merry way.
Walk in my purpose, live in expectation,
live my blessed life keeping the devil at bay.

It's very hard to watch the woes and
vulgarity of what's happening to
civilization.
As we are children of the Most High King
we have fallen short of our agnation.
It hurts my heart to see the lack of God's
children not understanding their salvation.

This thing about free will has taken Its toll,
He is the only Way, the Truth, and the
Light.
Don't want to be in a position to miss my
blessing and God and all His delight.
It never hurt anyone to be kind, love one
another, and just plain be polite.

Ode to my mom

The most beautiful person I have known
inside and out.
Caring, giving, charming, steadfast, and a
diplomat no doubt.
She was born one fine day in the month of
May to be exact.
I am sure the Heavens and earth had no
choice but to react.

She lived a life of grandeur, poise and quite
a bit of pomp and circumstance.
There was very little room for error in her
children's lives but somehow, we always got
another chance.

July 4th is a national holiday of
independence.
But God, in His infinite wisdom,
gave her one more day for her
surrenderance.

July 5th is a day that pierced my heart and rocked My soul.
If you look close enough you can still see the hole.

I loved my mom and I miss her still.
I know that she is in God's hands and that it was His will.

She has been gone for some time now.
I'm still coming to terms with it I just don't know how.
They say it gets easier, not sure that's correct.
I thank God for You Jesus and my heart that You protect.

Ode to Rebecca Price, Bailey Patterson.
    An angel that earth could not keep and
    Heaven adores, your work is all done.
    I can't wait to see you again.
    On the golden streets of Heaven where
    we can really get it in!

Conclusion of the Matter

I wish I could wave a wand or do something *very* clever,
Then all the things in my life would seem to
be a little better.

Times I think all ducks are in a row and I'm
in a good place.
Here comes a reason to check myself l fall
down on my face.

The reality is that God is still Alpha and
Omega, large and in control.
He has the last words of every story that's
ever been told.

So, I'll do what the Bible instructs me
to and pray some more.
When everything is falling apart and
I'm hurt to my core.
Wow!

There is tragedy all around. Oh boy!
How I've cried, folks are having problems
galore.

Time is not ours to keep, waiting for no
one, it's getting short.
Stop! Grudges, hatred, or disenchantment
it's time to abort.

Today, if it were not for Jesus, I would be
more than just sad.
Because of the God I serve I can live,
rejoice, and be glad.

Some have even died, but God, not a man
that can lie does not make a mistake.
Blessed are we to trust in Him so our hearts
do not break.

It may be hard times, for us today or in
this minute.
Be joyful and have pleasure we're not
alone, He is always in it.

God doesn't do things our way, only good things in His heart.

Day by day new mercies He gives let us give praise, honor, glory to God for a brand-new start.

Only what you do
For God will last

Only what we do for God is going to last.
Anything else will quickly be a thing
of our past.

We have no idea when our day begins and
we get started.
How important it is to keep our eye and ear
gates guarded.

Had it not been for that day and a tree on
the hill.
We would be doomed to Hell and not know
God's will.

Either we make up our minds to follow
Him.
Sooner or later we will find ourselves
out on a limb.

Only what we do for God is going to last.
He is a great and wonderful God, to please
Him is a blast.

He has only asked us to love one another
like He loves us.
And not to sit around making excuses about
how to adjust.

We are His people and the sheep of His
pasture.
All we need to do is what we can to obey
the Master.

            1 Corinthians 15:58

What God Said

Come, listen, and follow Me. I have so much to Tell you and will never lead you astray.
Don't you dare listen to the devil with all his Cunning ways. He has nothing good to say.

I have come that you would have a good life and Life more abundant.
Remember that we don't fight against flesh and Blood but the devil incumbent.

There are many things I wish for you to know, be Still and lend me your ear.
I am going to redeem you and take away all that displeases me but of the devil you must stay clear.

You, My loves, spend too much time about what you can't see.

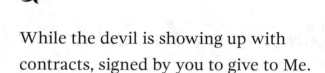

While the devil is showing up with contracts, signed by you to give to Me.

What, My children, will it take for you to understand that day at Calvary?
I bled and died for all your sins, and beat the devil at his game, as I hung upon that tree.

You are heirs of the Kingdom seated in heavenly places with me and the Father.
Don't let yourself be taken with the devil. He will take your life and treat it like he is a master carver.

I want you to know that you are fearfully and wonderfully made in My image, the King of Kings.
Resist the devil, he will flee from you. Come, come home swiftly I will hide you under My wings.

Love, salvation, redemption, and forgiveness, is your portion—a gift from Me to you.
Stay on that narrow path that averts the devil.
It will bring you straight to Me, without any further ado.

Whose we are

Come on people of God let's be who we really are.
We don't have to sit and wonder or wish upon a star.

We are sons and daughters of the Most High King.
When we think we are in trouble He will hide us beneath His wing.

There is no condemnation in this good life we've been given.
No good thing is withheld from us, no whip by which we're driven.

We are more than conquerors don't let it be misunderstood.
We are born to be gallant soldiers in a royal priest hood.

We are above and not beneath, blessed
going in, blessed going out, blessed in the
city blessed in the field.
Wearing our royal garments, yes, we are
dressed To impress, and don't forget dear
Calvary there is A note upon your shield.

We are handed love, grace and favor to
carry us through our days.
We only need to say to Him, "I love you
Lord. How do we count the ways?"

We are a peculiar people, His plan and
purpose for sure.
To set us apart from all the rest, to give us
confidence to endure.

What do we say to ourselves
knowing in Him we can do all
things?
He gives us strengths and comforts
us, each day new joy and mercy He
brings.

What more could we possibly ask for when we're as privileged as can be.
Okay I know the answer! Jesus keep me nearer my God to Thee.

Humble yourself
Or you will fail

E're body out here on a hustle and flow.
Sure ain't nobody on the down low no
mo.
In the church and out the back door.

People doing anything and everything to
get that coin.
Even satan ranks they will join.

Humble your self or you will fail.
Perhaps even end up in jail.

Seems everyone on a street car name
desire.
Stealing young girls and boys, setting
them up for hire.

How long do we think God will let this
go on? Have we forgotten all about
what the good book is saying?

Everybody is a wanna be or trying to be a
boss, is anybody really still praying.

Humble yourself or you will fail.
Never mind about having all the duckets in
your pail.

This is the time to check the move of God.
You don't want no part of the devil's fraud.

We outcher, yes we are!
In the clubs and at the bar.
In the office until midnight trying to be a
rockstar.

When do we have a clear moment and say.
Whoops! No! It's about time I am going the
other way.
There is too high a price I've got to pay.

E're body wants to be in the main
thrust.
Whatever happened to in God we trust?

Humble yourself or you will fail.
This is not the place to derail.

Time has gone by and now it's completely
run out.
There is a shaking and a wakening that is
coming about.

We can't do nothing without God's
permission.
We wake up no day on our own volition.

Just thought I give that a mention.
We are in trouble as a nation.

E're body wants to be a sensation.
Lord have mercy on all Your
creation!

Plan and Purpose

We have got to begin to call a thing a thing.
Get out of God's way and get under His wing.

Do not claim any attack of the evil one.
He ain't had no juice since the world begun.

Let us give credit where credit is due.
Was it satan or Jesus who said he'd never leave you?

Come on people of God I have been as guilty as you.
Today is a new day. We can't stand for no more of this who do?
You do! Voodoo.

Our God is bigger and badder than all of satan's clan.

He is a God of restoration and all
possibilities and I know He can.
He holds the whole world in His hand.

Reach out let him know you trust and
believe.
He is able to do all He said He would do.
Are we willing to receive?

Can I get a witness to what it really is?
God will be back in a few it is no secret and
you don't have to be a whiz.

Get yourself a testimony.
Stand on a ceremony.

We have our own free will
Satan's job is to seek to kill.

Open up your heart.
Make a brand new start.

Don't you want a different life?
Without heart ache and strife.

Plan, purpose, and pursue
all that God has for you!

I know I know

I know! I know! *We were all born into sin.*
Keep doing the same things all over, and
over again.

I don't know why we believe living should
be such a hurried jaunt.
Trying to tear down the next person to get
Whatever we want.

We are joint-kingdom heirs.
There is no plane to catch, nor track to run
in God we should cast our cares.

We need to have full recall.
God has made provision for us all.

Its not about you and it's not about
me.
It was Jesus who hung on Calvary.

It will be Him who will make the final decision.
Why make our lives Hell or a temporary prison?

Take it slow and learn to know all we need is more finesse.
And much, much less selfishness.

Allow your conscience to be your guide.
Do what you can on earth in a holy stride.

We all have to come this way.
In God we should live and to Him we must pray.

Hello Fall

Fall is a time for hustle and bustle gratefulness and thanksgiving.
Whereby we all gather together blessed
that we are still living.

The leaves on the trees start turning to give
us a clue.
That life goes on no matter what we do.

Football games and wearing sweaters too is
all a part of the season you see.
Pumpkin and potatoes pies too, reds,
oranges, ambers and brown, is the color
palette to be found on the ground.

Doing back to school shopping; jeans,
hats, scarves, and a little light jacket.
College dorms filling up with students
making a whole lot of racket.

Switching out our wardrobes, replacing
halters with hoodies.
Sitting down doing homework with our
children, giving them snacks and other
goodies.

Squirrels in your back yard are making tree
holes their huts.
Flashing their bushy tails getting ready to
settle down, squandering for nuts.

As much as I will miss summer, no doubt.
Keeping it moving is what life is all about.

No more children running through the
park, cookouts, and outdoor dining.
Still we have bright mornings just a little
less sun is shining.

With the move of God's hand, we go from one season to the next.
Like it or not, it is what it is, the Creator you will respect.

It takes some longer than others to make the adjustment from summer to fall.
Thank You Lord for another season and reason to love You, praise You and give You my all.

Pray For Our Children

*W*hat will it take for us to really pray?
We see so much of the enemies
work each and everyday.

Has prayer become, in the hearts of men,
just a Thing of the past?
The Bible clearly tell us to go to God in
prayer and only what we do for God is what
is going to last.

Are we too busy about our own
business, jobs, And doing whatever
in this world?
That we have forgotten to pray and
teach each precious boy and girl.

We know that it is written that there would be times like this.
We're also told to watch and pray and be obedient to the Word, a fiery dart we would miss.

We are told to humble ourselves and pray and seek God's face.
Then God could save our children with His love and awesome grace.

Folks keep saying all the time how can we stop these senseless attacks and killings?
What part of getting on our knees and praying to God above that makes us so unwilling?

Now is the time to take our homes, cities, states And country back.
By not forsaking the assembly, praying without ceasing to get us back on track.

If we would come together as one for all
our children's good.
And teach them how to pray, perhaps
when they go outside they would not be so
misunderstood.

Which way

We are anointed before we are appointed.
Because God can't use us if we get disjointed.

We think we see the Forrest in the trees.
But when is the last time we were on our knees.

There is heavy price for us to pay.
To do the work of the Lord in this day.

Everybody got their peering eyes on you.
Like we are caged animals in the local zoo.

Let us be careful not to let the devil use our indwelling spirit.
Of course his only plan and job is to seek, destroy, and kill it.

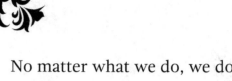

No matter what we do, we don't want to get on the wrong track.
Some of these trains leaving the station are not coming back.

We must keep our eyes pealed for devils barking Hell hounds.
God tells us to keep our mind on Him and our feet on solid grounds.

There is no where in Hell to be comfortable and live.
Satan is a defeated foe he don't have nothing but misery to give.

It is worth it all to keep our head, heart, and hands clean before the Lord.
Put our armor on everyday girded up for battle not forgetting our sword.

We must allow our hope to be in nothing
less,
than Jesus' love and righteousness.
Amen

Later for the hater

Not sure why we, the people of God, give our haters so much time or credence. Those people work for the devil, we all know to God he has no allegiance.

Come on now we have to stop giving them to much credit.
We should pray and ignore them.
Bother you don't let it.

They pray against your every moment.
They are Awake to plot your demise.
Really, we should not concern ourselves, God will ultimately make them their right size.

We know, we know better!
What on earth is the matter with us?
We are the people of God and in God we must trust.

They said it, you believe it, shame on you when there is no truth to it.
The job of the hater is to get a rise out of you, then they think they get the benefit.

They have so much to say with their slick talk and all.
Then you fight right back.
Then you too look small.

We must rise above all negativity.
The haters hate themselves more than they hate you.

> If it were not so they would
> get a life, praise God, and have
> something positive to do.

We turn out to be worse than our haters giving them an audience in our life.
God bless your hater, praying for you all the way to Heaven got no time for your strife.

When you are on team Jesus, you do as He would do, bless them and keep it moving.
Sticks and stones may break our bones but when you work for the devil your words are not behooving.

Some things are better left alone.
Anything a hater has to say to you, has no application.
If God be for you who can be against you?
When you do all things in prayer and supplication.

I know sometimes it is easier said than done.
Just put God first. He will do the rest.

Later for the hater, he belongs to God too.
Pray again and again, that he will pass
God's test.

We have such little time here to be the best
we can be.
Don't let nothing separate you from God's
love and His gift of eternity.

Time Out

I have learned to say thank You Jesus when
my feet hit the flo.
I don't want to be a player no mo.
I want the hand of God to lead and guide
me for sho.

As I look around at many things I've done.
Had nothing to do with God no not one.
Oh! I was all in and thought it was fun.

I have made up my mind and a
conscience Decision to serve Him.
Nothing, nobody can stop me Sally,
Jeffery, or Shaquita and nem.
Started to realize I wanted to go to
Heaven and at this rate my chances
were very slim.

This is not a walk of shame I walk today.
It is the road called, "The King's Highway."
I love where my journey has taken me.
I believe I'll stay.

I had the opportunity in the world and paid
my dues.
I'd like to put you up on some worldly
news.
The evil one's job is to steal, kill, and
accuse.

No, my playing with the devil days are no
more.
You can now find me working in God's
Kingdom for sure.
Put all that stuff behind me and closed the
door.
> Now! I give Him honor, glory, and
> praise.
> I am much, much happier these days.
> My life, my head is no longer in a
> haze.

This is the effect God's love has had on me.
I dare you to trust Him, then you too can
see.
Being a player isn't what is crocked up to
be.

Yes completely yes

Up all night praying. *God gave me a word* at the end of 2014 and he is bringing it to pass, so very close to home. People of God please come to Jesus before it's too late. All we have to do is say, "Yes Lord Yes!" Completely yes and He will do the rest.

He will not put you under arrest He is a perfect gentleman at best. Please, I hope it's not too late. Just give all to Jesus all of what's on your plate. Return back to God all He has blessed you with. Saying thank You, for His Son Jesus what a precious gift.

Believe in your whole heart that he died and rose again Shed His precious blood for my and your sin. Believe, in the Father, the Son, and the Holy Ghost.

No matter, in life who loves you, know God loves you the best and the most.

The Clarion Horn

As you free your mind,
you will free your time,
To ride on the glory line.

It takes but one good decision,
to get all your ducks in a row, with proper precision.
Choose the One who has all the provision.

We scour around from day to day.
Not giving thought to what we do or say.
We need to figure out that we are out of God's will and His way.

He cares for us,
Where is our trust?
To be in relationship with Him is a must.

Don't you want to live a life that is free?
Then we must start to declare and decree.
Only what we do for God is going to last.
Don't you see?

There is really nothing to think about.
When you come to know Jesus, you can't
help but shout.
Bottom line is He knew you from the
foundation of the earth no doubt.

Come one come all that are heavy laden.
This world we live in is ghastly fading.
God is calling for a mass repentance this
goes without stating.

Put your big girl/boy pants on and
don't be forlorn.
The darkness and the night are over, a
new day is born.

The devil is a liar.

We are children of the Most High King.

Let's sound the Clarion Horn!

Jesus is Lord!

Keep It Real

W hy can't we just keep it real?
So much smoke and mirrors what's
the deal?

It is what it is! Let it do what it do!
What part don't you understand, it's not
about you!

Tell the truth, let God love you, should be
your story.
End of the day God's going to get all
the glory.

Be yourself and in all you're getting
get understanding.
Best recipe for happy landing.

God-Appointment!

The Lord wants our attention.
Need I say more or not even mention.

Whatever we think is the matter?
It's only the evil one and his posse chatter.

We have been fearfully and wonderfully made.
It's up to us to make the grade.

Get in alignment.
With your assignment.

Elevate your life.
We're too blessed for strife.

He is only trying to tell us a story
of all His wonder and His glory.

Did I say this before or forgot to mention.
He sees us going to and fro.
Aimless not knowing which way to go.

Love the Lord don't hesitate.
Don't forget this appointment and don't be late.

The evil one

You believe that 45 is something, the way things are going he could have us all dead.

We are living in the last days.

Just wait until the Anti-Christ rears its ugly head.

The evil one is soon to come, believe you me it's a fact, because it is written.

No matter how many times you have been told he already has some of you smitten.

It is so important that we spend time and be Proactive in studying the Word.

It is told to us from the beginning of time put on your armor and carry your sword.

Important to know if the Bible says, it believe it. God's Word does not come back void.

Seeking first The Kingdom of God so that we
may live not die or ever be destroyed.

Stay prayed up in this difficult time, only
what we do for God is going to last.
Stay in God's will and in His way.
45 may not be the evil one but the die has
been cast.

Check one two
Drop the mic

It is a shame when you have to stay away *from* People you once knew.
Because they are so narrowed minded that all they can see is the jacked up them in you.

You work really hard to stay the course.
All they can offer is cynicism and remorse.

I have come too far to turn around.
Got my feet on some solid ground.
All I can do is pray my hardest that I will past the test because it seems to me that they are still bound.

Nothing and no one are going to separate me from the love of God.
No, not even you.
I got my orders from on high. I now belong to the "Jesus crew."

It is clear to me that you don't understand my plight.
My job in life is to love you not to engage you in the fight.

God has a plan for all of us, and I have taken up my cross.
I cannot help if you still want to serve the enemy, that's your loss.

Something else I would just like to say.
It may be a good thing for you to stop checking for me and get down on your knees to and pray.

My name is Connie Hemingway,
and I approve this message.

The blood of Jesus

Thank You, Jesus! We are trying to hold on to what we've got.
Because dear God, You gave it to us and we appreciate it a lot.

You died and rose again without a word.
How dare we go through life and not thank You, that would be totally absurd.

When we are confused and don't know which way to turn.
You offer us Your Word that we should learn.

No matter what it looks like and no matter what the people say.
If God said it, He is faithful to perform it. He is the Potter, and we are the clay.

Hold on to what you have this day.
Our Lord and Savior comes to give us more
of Him not to take away.

Be blessed of the Lord each and every one
of you. The day has come for you to rest.
The evil one's job: kill, and destroy has no
other mission than to put us to the test?

Jesus loves to give to His children, brothers
in sisters in Christ.
We have all that we need and could ever
ask for. The blood of Jesus we were bought
with a price.

Now that's love

They hung Him high and stretched Him wide, and then He died for you and I.
Now that's "LOVE"

They nailed one hand and then the other.
They nailed His feet called it defeat.
Now that's "LOVE"

They put thorns around His head.
Called it a crown stood over Him with their sword.
They lashed Him thoroughly He never said a word.
Believing they left Him for dead.
Now that's "LOVE"

But thanks be to God it did not end there.
He took on the sins of the world to bare.
"Forgive them," He said out loud.

Before the ones who still remained just a few
not a crowd.
Now that's "LOVE"

"It is finished," they heard Him say.
Was not the end all to be all that day.
Why have You forsaken Me?
Was only the beginning you see.
There is more to the story.
He shed His blood on Calvary.
That was a wake up call for me.
The grave could not hold Him and death had
no victory.
Now that is "LOVE"

On that third day our Savior got up to heal
the world.
Every man, woman, boy and girl.
I am so glad He lived, died, and got up
from the grave.
His passion, blood, stripes and tears
clothes, and Body full of blood stain.

It was all done for us to be saved.

His glory and mercy to attain.

Now that's "LOVE"

He got up

He got up after they made Him a crown
thorns and hitched Him to a tree.
He got up knowing that was not the end
that day on Calvary.

He got up from a grave closed shut with a
stone.
He got up and by all accounts there were
nails driven in His bone.

He got up after they lied, scorned,
ridiculed, and dragged him through
the street.
He got up to fulfill His reason for
being, only He could establish that
feat.

He got up and nobody could tell what had took place.
He got up because He was His Father's Son filled with love and grace.

He got up to be an example that any and all of our debts had been paid.
He got up went about His business and still He never swayed.

He got up at the crack of dawn, after three days with all power in His hand.
He got up after standing proxy for you and I just as was God's plan.

My Daddy Says, "Today"

We are to live a life of expectation!
For those of you who are hating,
instigating, and perpetrating, you need to
repent and have your time well-spent.
I am a God of love and restoration, and do
it with no hesitation.

I am calling the deep to the deep,
Not a bunch of know it all's in a heap.
If you have missed My call on your
life, renew your mind and rid it of
strife.

I am soon to come again,
For a church without spot, wrinkle,
or sin.
Now do what I have asked you to.
When I return, I will receive you.
I have established for you a life of
salvation.

Not for you to live a life of temptation.
Learn My ways,
and prolong your days.

Some of you stop trying to be Me.
You are a part of My inventory.
I will always get the glory.
I will bring all My promises to fruition.
Be a part of My commission not omission.

To God be the glory
That's why

Hey. Hey you know me. My name is Connie.

One of God's kids that at one time backslid.

I am on the right road today.

Came with fasting and I had to pray.

And God's steady hand when I refused to stand.

Oh it's good to be back home again.

Beats living a life of sin and all its disdain.

Thank You Lord for rescuing me from that wretched life.

When I didn't know I was in the throughs of filth and strife, I am feeling much better now about My new space.

Your loving kindness and unending grace,
has brought me a mighty, long way
from the muck and mire.
I am proud of myself today and most
grateful I missed that Hell fire.

To You, and You, alone I owe my life to.
Never would have made it a day without
You.

Can't nobody tell this story better than I.
You see I lived it and refuse to die.
To God be the glory—that's why.

One way

We look, but do we see?
There is only one way to glory.

We have our minds set on dreams and a
goal.
As if they were a fortune to be told.

Why is it so hard for us to get in the Word?
Instead of believing that it's absurd.

How do we know what day will be
our last?
This is why Jesus said on Him our
cares should be cast.

We are not living in a time of make
believe.
The struggle and the journey is real.
Is that so hard to conceive?

We all living on borrowed time by the grace.
Soon our time will be up in this place.

God inhabits the praises of His people, has our praise and prayer life been fervent?
Will we be able to hear, "Well done my good and faithful servant?"

There is much work to be done before the setting of the sun.

We don't want to be considered as vestige.
Let us adhere to the two signs with the same message.

One way back to the cross,
and to our Father in Heaven, He is the only BOSS.

Turn around your
Turnaround

He *walks with me and He talks with me* and tells me I am His own, hey Glory! Some people may not like this but that's okay.

This is one of the times you do what you are told. You do not have anything to say!

"Turnaround your Turnaround" isn't no messin' around. It's clear as the driven snow.
God got angles taking charge over you, just thought that you should know.

It's not sometime, onetime, two weeks ago, one day or on a Sunday.
Not like sitting around either waiting on your bae.

It's every day, all day His wonders do not cease.
Our job is to accept what we have and He will Supply the increase.

In the amphitheater and marketplace we call the "world," things happen and do take place.
Each one with their cares and woes to bear should learn to seek God's face.

If we only understood the price that He paid.
We would not have to worry about who smashed the homey on love in the afternoon, where the gangs are meeting tonight, or who got made.

There would be no thought for tomorrow.
Your today would be just fine.
When you know and believe in Jesus right straight down in your core,

your "turnaround" isn't no mess around it's
clear as the driven snow.
I pray these words will help some
"turnaround" and knock on Jesus' door.

You don't have to feel better to do better
you are already the best.
We're so busy moseying around the crib, or
going hard for the streets, and all He really
wants for us is to abide in Him and obey
Him, and take our rest.

Don't be the one to "turnaround" and find
Yourself in a mess.
Your "turnaround" isn't no mess
around it's clear as the driven snow.
Depending on who you know, King
Jesus the Author and Finisher of
your faith.

No fight, just love

I don't live the life of a kangaroo, don't intend to box or fight with any of you, get your life, trust God, and He will see you thru.

Some of us living all wrong — straight bogus.
Nothing out here belongs to us.
It's not about you or me, but Jesus.

Take your attitude and turn it around.
That's if you intend to be Heaven-bound.
Love must be a part of your glory crown.

It only takes but a minute to be kind to someone.
It takes a lifetime when you hate.
It will have you undone.
We must not live a life cunning and on the run.

Remember it was Jesus that died on
Calvary.
He already defeated the devil that's not for
you or me.
There is no need to fight with your
neighbor, can't you see.

We are the keeper of each other.
Let us love and be kind to one another.

Be with Him today

God has given me a job to do.
It has to do with! Him, me, and you.

He ask me to tell you that He is coming
back, before long.
You will witness His splendor mighty and
strong.

We can't be certain of the day or hour.
But we mustn't give up for He has given us
His power.

There is nothing that we do that He does
not know about us.
All He asks is that we have the ability to
obedient, believe, love, and trust.

This thing called life has no reason or rhyme.

He just wants us all to know we are running out of time.

To say yes Lord to Your will and to Your way.

Won't you come and be with Him today.

The Word of The Lord...

Can't measure it
Just treasure it

Two thousand twenty.
The year of devastation a plenty.

But when I think about all that God has
done for me.
And where He brought me from as far as
from Hell to a life of eternity.

He took the cussing out of my mouth, the
whisky out of my veins.
Gave me a new set of clothes took away the
old ones full of stains.

I don't have time to tell you all of what He
has brought me through.
Just take my word for it. If He did it for me
He will do it for you.

When we come to terms with, we are
nothing without Him and His love.
We can begin to set our sights on the things
from up above.

There is nothing for us to do but to put our
hands together,
and place many thank You's on our lips
because He has been there no matter
whatever.

Can I get a witness? Do you have that
spiritual connection?
Behold the Lamb of God we are
going in the right direction.

If we lift Him up like we put others
down,
we will find our life as that of a
survivor and not one that's about to
drown.

There is no life like that of living in the knowledge that God has your back.
It will take you to new dimensions where there is no lack.

When I think about His tenderness and how with just the touch of His hand,
We will find ourselves in a better place, the salt of the earth, and not in sinking sand.

I use to be on the wrong road going about 100 miles an hour.
And He looked beyond my faults and delivered me with His power.

Thank You Lord this is your humble servant and to You be all the glory!

Jesus is coming back

I can write you a story. I could sing you a song.
Jesus is coming back and it won't be long.

He has plans and purposes for your life and mine.
Don't be finger popping and bar hopping and get left behind.

Talking trash and trying to bash your fellow man.
My Lord don't like none of that. No, He is not a fan.

Pay attention to your surroundings.
I suggest you do.
You ask, "who me?" Yes. I'm talking to you!

Jesus is coming back, and it won't be long.
Nearer my God to Thee should be your
favorite song.

We must put our body, mind, and soul in
check.
Get our heads out of the gutter and of each
other to benign and give God some respect.

Jesus is coming back, and it won't be long.
Repent! Get God's words now shut up in
your bones.
Get out of the streets, TV, and stop all your
gossiping on the newest cell phones.

Jesus is coming back, and it won't be long.
He has plans and purposes for you and for
your life and mine.
    We are living in times that are very
    trying, the evil spirits of darkness are
    to be bind.

Now, I have written you a story and sang
you a song.
God is coming back, and it won't be long.

Get your business fixed!
Don't fall for the devil's tricks!

Get yourself right with Him!
You are a precious gem!

Know that He is God!
Plant your seeds in fertile sod!

Don't let the devil win!
Come out of all your sin!

To God be the Glory!

Chop Chop !

No time for the blues.
Get on God's bus and take a cruise.

He will take you from point A to point Z.
We just have to be sure to give Him the
praise, honor, and glory.

There is no fare. The ride is free.
All you have to do is show up in victory.

Bus stops at all destinations.
Stay on if you feel any hesitations.

He will never leave you or forsake you.
The more you ride, the more you get
   instructions and power to see you thru.

   Come take a ride on God's bus with me
   today.

Relax and get ready for whatever comes your way.

While riding, He will take away all your trouble.
Blessings will be your destination at the end of the day, you will receive double.

I pray that all will come on board and enjoy the ride.
He is irrespective of persons, and He will never leave your side.

What concerns us, concerns Him as well.
Make sure you are on God's bus. All others are going to Hell!

Getting on the
Good foot

There is a blessing in the pressing,
and a lesson in the progression.

Stay in God's will.
Stand and be still.

He is the secret place.
The One we want to chase.

You have to be armed with forgiveness .
To be about our Father's business.

Jesus is the Way, the Light of the World.
He shines brightly for every boy and girl.

If Kingdom work is your aim and
purpose.
Make yourself familiar with the good
book verses.

Yes there are some things He is preparing us for.
Can open and close what looks like an impossible door.

Let us seek to have the mind of Christ.
And not live life like a game of dice.

Continue to look to the hills where our help comes from.
We are not to live a life of ho-hum drum.

Clean us up Lord, from all that is not pure.
Give us your love and strength to endure.

Getting on the Good Foot is what we need to be about.
Thank the Lord for His new mercies let's praise, let's shout!

CPSIA information can be obtained
at www.ICGtesting.com
Printed in the USA
BVHW041432160621
609642BV00005B/1337